The FIRST BOOK of
VOLCANOES AND EARTHQUAKES

The FIRST BOOK of

VOLCANOES

and

EARTHQUAKES

13,055

by Rebecca B. Marcus

ILLUSTRATED WITH PHOTOGRAPHS AND DIAGRAMS

FRANKLIN WATTS, INC.
575 Lexington Avenue • New York 22

SBN 531-00661-1

7   8

Contents

A Cornfield Erupts into Fame   1

A Research Laboratory Supplied by Nature   2

What Is a Volcano?   3

Enough Heat to Melt Metals   4

The Important Part Pressure Plays   6

When Magma Breaks Through . . .   7

Weak Spots in the Earth's Crust   8

Trace Your Finger Along the Volcanic Belts   10

Different Magmas Cause Different Eruptions   12

Plateaus of Lava Rock   13

Gases from a Volcano's Vent   14

Showers of Hot Rocks   16

When Lava Flows   17

Strange Lava Forms   19

A Glass Mountain, and Rock That Floats   23

The Shapes of Volcanic Cones   25

Craters Vary, Too   27

How Volcanologists Use Their Knowledge   29

People Make Use of Eruptions   30

Hot Springs   31

A Special Kind of Hot Spring   32

Earthquakes Can Change the Face of the Earth   36

When the Solid Rock Shifts   37

Shock Waves Set Off by Earthquakes   39

The All-Important Seismometer   40

Pinpointing an Earthquake   46

A Seismometer Has Other Uses, Too   49

When an Earthquake Strikes   51

Glossary   57

Index   61

Paricutín at night during eruption.

Paricutín Volcano erupting in daylight.

A Cornfield Erupts into Fame

As A Mexican farmer named Dionisio Pulido was plowing his cornfield on February 20, 1943, he noticed that the ground under his bare feet felt unnaturally warm. This struck him as strange — just as strange as the rumblings that had been coming from under the earth for the last two weeks. But since early spring planting-time was near, Pulido continued to prepare his soil for seeding. Suddenly, to his astonishment, a patch of ground collapsed near his feet. The rumbling became a roar, and a column of white smoke rose from a crack that appeared in the ground. Soon a tremendous explosion tore through the patch which had just sunk. Dust, rocks, and great black clouds were thrown many hundreds of feet into the air.

Terrified, the Mexican farmer rushed to the nearby village of Paricutín to tell his neighbors of the dreadful things happening in his cornfield. But by the time Pulido arrived, they had already heard the noise of the explosion and had seen the black clouds. In panic, they were piling their belongings into carts and onto their burros, and preparing to flee for their lives.

All night, the dark sky and the surrounding countryside were lit up by fiery rocks and ashes erupting from the hole in the ground, as if by a giant display of fireworks. Up, up went the red-hot rocks and ashes, more than a thousand feet toward the sky. Then they fell back, to pile up around the opening from which they had come. By the next morning, a blunt, cone-shaped hill 120 feet high was standing where a level field had been only the day before.

A volcano had just been born!

News of the birth of this volcano was immediately flashed from the little town of Paricutín to the outside world. Dionisio Pulido's cornfield became famous overnight.

1

A Research Laboratory Supplied by Nature

THREE DAYS after its birth, volcanologists — scientists who study volcanoes — had already arrived in Paricutín to study at first hand how a volcano is born. It was an opportunity they might never have again, for although there were a few records in history of the beginnings of new volcanoes, no real on-the-spot study of them had ever been made. Now nature had supplied a research laboratory such as volcanologists had scarcely dreamed of having.

These scientists made notes of the material thrust out by the new volcano. They measured the temperature of the molten rock, or *lava*, which had begun to flow out of a crack in the volcano, as well as how fast this lava flowed. They also observed carefully how lava cemented the loose rocks together into a solid mass. All of this information, together with that discovered from other volcanoes, helped to give them a better knowledge of all volcanic activity and of the interior of the earth as well.

As for Paricutín Volcano itself, it continued to erupt violently and to expel large amounts of rock and lava for about four years before slowing down. By 1952, it had stopped erupting altogether, and scientists now believe it to be a "dead" volcano. During its life, it had built up a mountain some 1,400 feet high and several miles in diameter at its base. Although in that time much property had been destroyed, only one person had been injured.

While Paricutín was still erupting, people came from far and wide to watch it in action. If, however, you were to travel there today, all you would find would be a blunt, cone-shaped mountain and desolate fields covered with rock, ash, and hardened lava.

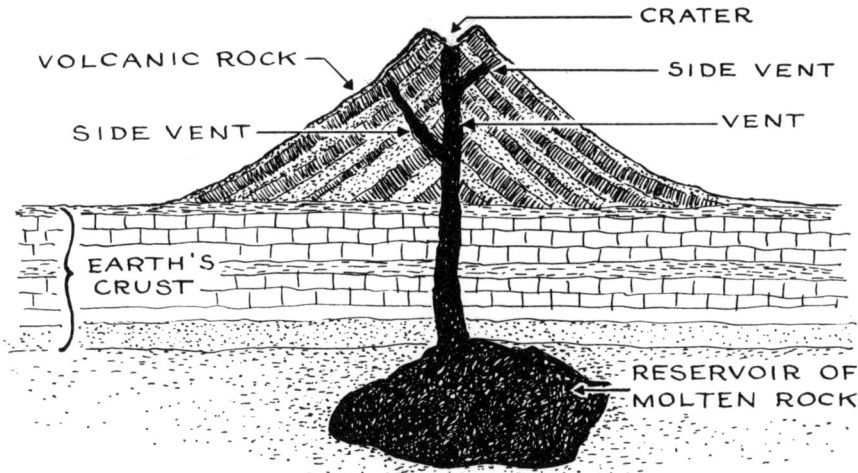

CRATER

VOLCANIC ROCK —

SIDE VENT

SIDE VENT —

VENT

EARTH'S CRUST

RESERVOIR OF MOLTEN ROCK

What Is a Volcano?

MOST MOUNTAINS that you are likely to see are not volcanoes. They were probably made by the uplifting of great blocks of the earth's crust, or by the crumpling and wrinkling of the crust. A volcano is a special kind of mountain. You might say that a volcano "built itself" from hot rocks or lava, or both, which came out of an opening in the ground as they did at Paricutín. Volcanoes usually look like cones with bowl-shaped depressions called *craters* at their tops. But what makes a volcano really different from any other mountain is the opening, or *vent*, which leads from the crater to an underground reservoir of molten rock.

Where did the heat come from to melt this rock?

3

Enough Heat to Melt Metals

ANCIENT PEOPLE did not know much about *volcanology*, the science of volcanoes. The early Romans believed that Vulcan, who was the god of fire and of metals, had his blacksmith's shops beneath certain mountains. They thought that these mountains, out of which flew smoke and sparks, were the chimneys of his workshops. One mountain in particular, on an island near Sicily, they claimed was the chimney of Vulcan's main workshop. The noises and rumblings coming from underground, said the Romans, were the banging of Vulcan's hammer against the anvil as he forged metals. The Romans called this island "Vulcano." Although Vulcano is not an important island, nor its mountain a very active volcano, its name became our word "volcano." And it is this word that we now use for any mountain that expels hot rock, lava, or gases.

In one way, the ancients were correct. It may not be Vulcan's forges that lie underground, but we do know that there is enough heat inside the earth to melt metals and rocks. In fact, there is more heat there than any Roman could possibly have imagined. And although no one has ever been able to dig many miles below the earth's surface, scientists do know something about the material that makes up our planet's interior. They have learned this by studying the way in which earthquake shock waves — about which you will learn later — travel through the earth.

According to what is known at present, scientists believe that the *crust* — the first 20 or 30 miles down toward the earth's center — is made of rock very much like the granite and basalt rock we find on the surface. Below this crust, the next 1,800 miles — known as the *mantle* — is solid rock of a different type; it is rich in iron and other minerals. The last 2,000 miles or so — called the *core* — is made up of two zones. The outer zone is a very thick liquid or plastic-like rock, probably mostly

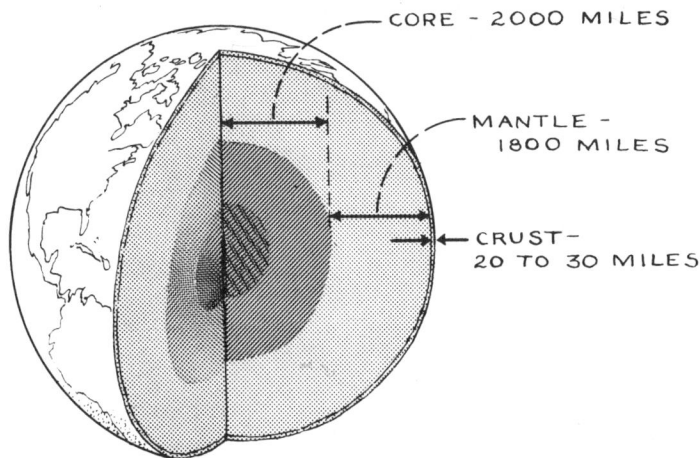

CORE - 2000 MILES

MANTLE -
1800 MILES

CRUST-
20 TO 30 MILES

iron, nickel, and cobalt. The inner zone is believed to be solid rock of the same material.

The interior of the earth is so hot that you would expect *all* the rock to be liquid. Imagine how hot it must be if — as scientists have figured — for the first few miles down, at least, the heat increases approximately 150 degrees for every mile! Of course, the heat cannot continue to increase at that rate, for if it did, the core would be hotter than the sun. Scientists believe that the core is from 4,000 to 8,000 degrees Fahrenheit.

It is also believed that there are three main sources of this heat. First, some of it still remains from the time when our earth was young and probably very hot. Second, the weight of the rock forming the upper layers is so great that more heat is produced deep down in the earth just from the tremendous pressure alone. Lastly, there are radioactive chemicals in the earth which regularly break down into other chemicals, and give off a great deal of heat in doing so.

5

Taken all together, these three sources surely provide enough heat inside the earth to melt rocks and minerals. And yet, in spite of this extreme heat, the material in the outer 1,800 miles has not melted. To understand why this is so, you must first know what is meant by "melting."

The Important Part Pressure Plays

To BEGIN WITH, all matter is made up of tiny particles called *molecules*, which are always in motion. In a solid substance, these molecules are packed together so closely that they can barely stir. However, when they are heated, they move faster and faster, and if there is enough room, they will move away from each other a little. We then say that the material is "expanding with heat." With the right amount of heat, the molecules will pull away from each other enough to make the solid material lose its shape and start to flow. We then say that "the solid is melting."

But now suppose that the pressure on the molecules is so great that they can hardly move at all — in spite of the heat. Then there is no room for them to push away from each other. In other words, the rock cannot expand and melt, and must remain in its solid state. Scientists have estimated that ten miles below the surface of the earth, the pressure on every square inch of rock is as great as 70,000 pounds! Little wonder, then, that most of our earth remains a mass of hard rock. Only at the outer core, almost 2,000 miles down, where the temperature is extremely high, can the rock material remain in a liquid state. But the heat at the inner core is still not high enough to permit melting, because of the greater pressure there.

Nevertheless, within the twenty or thirty miles of crust, some of the rock *does* melt and in time breaks through to the earth's surface. What makes this possible?

6

Volcanologists do not know for certain why, despite this tremendous pressure, rock can still become liquid, but they have several theories to explain the phenomenon. Here are the most important of them:

1. There may be many radioactive chemicals collected in certain areas, so that an unusual amount of heat is produced.

2. The weight of the rock above some places may be less than in others, due to the kind of material of which the rock is made. In such areas, the pressure may therefore not be great enough to prevent melting.

3. The earth's crust may be shrinking and wrinkling upward, releasing part of the pressure underneath. Under such conditions, melting could take place, too.

4. From time to time, great blocks of the earth's crust, weighing millions of tons, shift their positions. In doing so, they sometimes leave less pressure on the rock beneath them, and thus permit melting to take place.

In any or all of these ways, some of the once-solid rock in the interior of the earth becomes liquid, carrying steam and other gases dissolved in it. This substance is called *magma* as long as it remains underground, but *lava* when it appears above ground. Because magma is a liquid, it can squeeze its way through cracks in solid rock until it reaches a pocket in which it collects. There it remains until conditions are possible for it to break through to the earth's surface.

When Magma Breaks Through...

ONCE AGAIN, the right conditions for magma breakthrough are caused mostly by released pressure. First, as magma squeezes its way upward, the pressure on it decreases because there is less rock above it. Some of the dissolved steam and gases are then able to break into bubbles which,

7

as the pressure on them becomes even less, expand and burst. The bubbles usually burst with such force that they push magma along with the escaping gas. You can imagine how this occurs if you think of what happens when you quickly take the cap off a bottle of warm soda water. Pop! The gas imprisoned in the water suddenly rushes out, carrying some water along with it.

Volcanologists think this release of underground pressure is caused by the shifting of blocks of the earth's crust. Just as this shift in position may change the pressure, enabling rocks to melt, so it also lessens the pressure to make it possible for gas bubbles to propel the magma onward and upward. Then, if magma happens to lie in a weak part of the earth's crust, the force of the expanding gas may push it right through to the surface.

Weak Spots in the Earth's Crust

GEOLOGISTS have been able to locate these weak spots in the earth's crust to show where a volcano is likely to occur. The accompanying map tells you where they are located.

Notice that many of these weak spots are actually islands in the Pacific Ocean. Probably many of these islands started out as small volcanoes on the ocean floor, and then grew big enough to show above the water. In fact, we know that there are still many small volcanoes on the ocean floor. The most famous example of large volcanic islands is the Hawaiian Islands, which stretch out for about 1,500 miles in a band along a weakness in the earth's crust. You probably know the names of other volcanic islands in the Pacific — without realizing that they are really the tops of underwater volcanoes. Iwo Jima, Samoa, and the Midway Islands are only a few of them. There are many small ones dotting the ocean all the way from New Zealand to Hawaii.

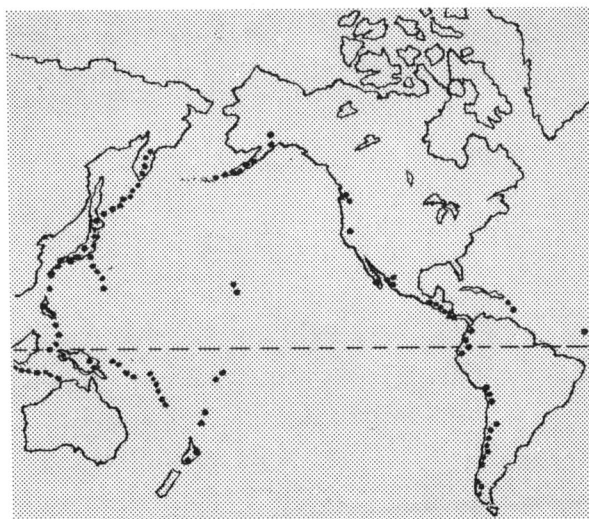

The earth's major volcanic zones.

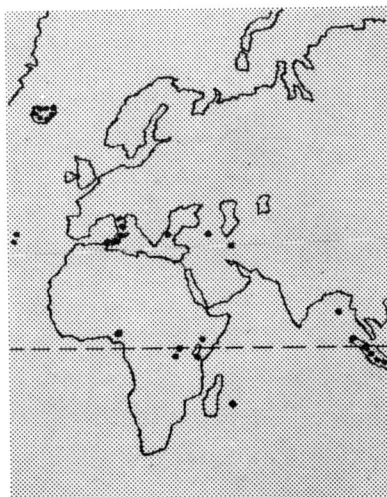

You can see, too, that there are many weak spots located along the edges of the continents which border the Pacific Ocean. There are so many active volcanoes in this area circling the ocean that the land along its edges has been called the "Pacific Belt of Fire."

Trace Your Finger Along the Volcanic Belts

LOOK AT THE MAP again and follow this "belt of fire." Start at Alaska and trace your finger westward. You can see a number of volcanoes in Alaska. Then, going across the water gap into Asia and southward, you come to Siberia, Japan, the Philippines, Indonesia, and New Zealand. The "belt of fire" then disappears under the ocean, but shows up again in the tip of South America. Now trace the belt northward close along the Pacific coast through the Andes Mountains, then up to Central America and Mexico. There the belt breaks, for between Mexico and Alaska there is only one known volcano, Mt. Lassen in California.

While there are other volcanic belts on our earth, these are not as big as the "Pacific Belt of Fire." On the Atlantic coast proper there are practically none, but notice the belt of volcanoes in the West Indies. The most famous of these is Mt. Pelée, on the island of Martinique, which, during its eruption in 1902, destroyed the city of St. Pierre.

Farther on, in the Atlantic Ocean, is yet another weak belt in the crust. Beginning with Iceland in the north, bring your finger southward to the Azores, the Canary Islands, the Cape Verde Islands, Ascension Island, St. Helena, and thence to Tristan da Cunha in the South Atlantic. Antarctica, too, has an active volcano. There are also a few other volcanic belts that run in a generally east-west direction. One of them cuts across Mexico, in the area where Paricutín is located. The land around the Mediterranean Sea lies in such a volcanic belt, too. Here you can find Mt. Vesuvius, Mt. Etna, Stromboli, and Vulcano. In ad-

Mt. Erebus, the active volcano in Antarctica.

Mt. Vesuvius in eruption.

dition, there is a weak belt in the earth's crust in central Africa. Added all together, about five hundred active volcanoes are now known, almost all of them lying in one or another of these volcanic belts.

Different Magmas Cause Different Eruptions

WHEN WE think of a volcanic eruption, we usually think of a mountain from which hot rocky material, steam, and other gases are thrust out of a crater with great force. Although many volcanoes do erupt in this way, there are others that pour out their lava quietly. The clue as to why a volcano erupts violently or quietly can be found in the kind of magma which will finally become the lava pouring through the volcano's vent.

There are two main families of magma: the granite family and the basalt family. Granite magma is made of light-colored rock, and is not as heavy as basalt magma. However, it is very sticky and flows more slowly. Scientists say that granite-type magma is more *viscous* than the basalt-type.

Because it is so viscous, this granite-type magma is able to hold a great deal of gas and steam imprisoned in it. As the magma reaches close to the surface, the gases and steam begin to escape. If, as often happens, the volcano's vent is plugged up with hardened lava, these gases remain trapped underground for a while. There they accumulate until enough gas pressure is built up to make it possible for them to force their way out of the vent. In doing so, they usually break up the rock material that plugged the vent, thrusting the fragments, together with bits of hardened magma, high into the air. Such an eruption is called an *explosive* eruption.

Basalt magma, on the other hand, is dark-colored and heavy. However, in spite of its greater weight, it flows more easily — or is more fluid — than molten granite. Another way to say this is to call basalt magma less *viscous* than granite magma. Because it is more fluid, steam and other gases can escape more readily from it while it is still underground. These gases, therefore, do not become bottled up beneath the ground, finally to burst out with explosive force. Also, when basalt magma reaches the surface, the lava is usually fluid enough to flow away from the vent before it hardens and closes up the opening. Basalt magma, then, usually causes a *quiet* eruption. The volcanoes of Hawaii erupt in this way, and have given the name "Hawaiian type" of eruption to this kind of lava flow.

Plateaus of Lava Rock

MANY QUIET lava flows of the past never built up mountains at all, because they did not erupt through deep, small, narrow openings in the earth's crust. Instead, the lava came through long cracks, or *fissures*, in the crust, and spread out like a sheet over large areas of land.

Such *fissure flows*, as they are called, are almost always of basalt-type lava. They built up the great plateaus of Iceland, the Deccan Plateau in India, the plateau of central Africa, and the Columbia River Plateau in our western states of Washington, Oregon, and Idaho. Fissure flows of the granite-type lava, called *rhyolite*, occurred in some parts of South America and in Yellowstone Park in Wyoming.

The greatest fissure flow of which there is any record in history took place in Iceland in the summer of 1783. At that time a crevice twenty miles long suddenly opened up, and out poured large amounts of lava, which soon covered an area of over two hundred square miles. Stories are still told by descendants of the people living at that time, of how the lava crept over the land, buried farms and homes, and changed the courses of rivers.

Fumaroles in New Zealand.

Gases from a Volcano's Vent

As WE KNOW already, when a volcano erupts it expels gases, pieces of rock, and lava. Let us find out more about these materials.

About a four-fifths part of all gases coming out of a volcano consists of steam. There is so much of it that it usually gives an eruption its explosive force. Other gases coming from volcanoes at one time or another are poisonous, and some, like sulfur dioxide and hydrogen sulfide, are evil-smelling besides. In some places, these gases come out of simple openings in the ground, called *fumaroles*. A number of fumaroles are usually found in the same area, as in Yellowstone National Park and in the Valley of Ten Thousand Smokes near Mt. Katmai in Alaska. It is a weird sensation indeed to walk on ground that is steaming all around you, as it does in these two national preserves!

14

Volcanic gases sometimes cause as much damage as burning-hot lava or hot pieces of rock. When they settle over an area, even for a short time, they leave behind them withered crops and dead livestock. People, too, can be smothered by these volcanic fumes. When Mt. Vesuvius erupted in 79 A.D., many of the people living in Pompeii at the foot of the volcano were suffocated or poisoned by gases issuing from it.

But all escaping volcanic gases are not harmful. Sometimes they carry along with them many useful metals such as lead, zinc, copper, tin, mercury, silver, and even gold. Then, as the gases erupt and lose their force, they deposit these minerals, often in the vent or *throat* of the volcano. A good example of such deposits are the gold and silver ores of Cripple Creek, Colorado, which were discovered to be in the throat of an ancient volcano.

Excavated ruins of Pompeii with Mt. Vesuvius in background.

Sometimes diamonds are found in the throat of an old, extinct volcano. In this case, however, the precious stone formed in the magma itself when hot carbon cooled slowly while under great pressure. During an eruption, it was carried to the throat by the magma and embedded there. The Kimberly diamond mines in South Africa — the most famous in the world — are in the throat of an old volcano. Indeed, these mines are often called the "diamond pipes of South Africa."

Showers of Hot Rocks

ALTHOUGH all these valuable materials are the result of eruptions, we cannot truly say they have been "ejected" or thrown out of a volcano. Rather, we would be more correct in saying that they were "deposited by volcanic action." We can, however, say that solid pieces of rock are ejected during an eruption. In trying to describe these solid rock materials accurately, scientists have found it useful to divide them into groups according to size.

The very finest powdery material is called, as you might expect, *dust*. The wind often blows this volcanic dust over great distances, far from its source. Volcanic dust can remain in the air for years after it has been ejected. When it is present in the atmosphere, it causes beautiful sunsets, as dust from Mt. Katmai did in 1912.

The pieces of solid volcanic material next larger in size, up to one quarter of an inch, are called *ash*. Then come *lapilli*, the Latin word for "little stones." Sometimes the word "cinders" is used in speaking of volcanic ash and lapilli. *Blocks* are hurled out from volcanoes as solid chunks of rock. They may be pieces torn from the sides of the crater, from the volcanic vent, or from a hardened crust of lava in the crater. They are sometimes tremendous in size. One such block, weighing two tons, was hurled from Stromboli for a distance of more than two miles from the crater!

Diamond mines of South Africa in the throat of an extinct volcano.

When Lava Flows

WHEN LAVA first flows from the volcano, it is so hot that it glows red or white, just as molten iron does when it comes out of a blast furnace. How fast it flows depends, of course, upon how steep the mountain is and how liquid the lava itself is. Usually, it flows about five miles an hour, but it has also been known to flow as fast as ten miles an hour.

17

Lava from Mt. Vesuvius engulfing San Sebastian, April, 1944.

Scientists have sometimes been able to change its path, as happened on the island of Hawaii in 1935. At that time Mauna Loa, a Hawaiian volcano, erupted, sending tongues of lava down its sides toward the city of Hilo. The city officials knew that previously, in 1881, such a lava flow had fortunately stopped just outside the city, but they decided not to trust to luck this time. Instead, they called upon geologists for help.

The geologists made a quick study of the flow, and then asked the United States Navy for cooperation. Before the tongue of lava reached the city, Air Force bombers dropped explosives in the path of the lava in such a way that the whole direction of the flow was changed. The city was saved.

Strange Lava Forms

PEOPLE WHO are able to find a place near enough and safe enough to watch lava flow, sometimes see it disappear through a crack into the ground. Then, as much as a mile or two farther down the slope, it emerges once more to the surface. It had just disappeared awhile into a tunnel.

The tunnel had been made earlier by a particularly slow lava flow. Rolling slowly down the mountain, the top of the lava cooled and hardened into a crust, while underneath it remained fluid and continued onward. When the supply of lava stopped coming from the crater, hot molten rock still flowed under the crust, somewhat as water flows in a hose for a while after the faucet has been turned off. Then it, too, cooled and hardened lower down the mountain, leaving behind it a tunnel whose roof was just-hardened crust. It is into such tunnels that lava from a new eruption sometimes disappears.

Lava tunnel in Craters of the Moon National Monument.

Union Pacific Railroad

Long, narrow caves in lava rock are also made in the same way, when a crust hardens and the lava underneath it then flows away. Craters of the Moon National Monument in Idaho has a number of such caves, some as wide as thirty feet across and a hundred feet long. But the island of Hawaii has more lava caves than any other place scientists know of. Mauna Loa has hundreds of them underneath its surface, as well as a great many tunnels. Should you ever visit Hawaii National Park, you will be able to go through some of them.

Sometimes lava cools and forms ground so jagged that it is hard to walk on and cannot be used for anything at all. At other times it has a fairly smooth surface, but even this is not really smooth. When you look at it, it makes you think of sticky tar which was poured out of a barrel while still hot, and then hardened. This smooth lava may harden into masses that look like many thick strands of rope. As you might expect, it is called *ropy* or *corded* lava.

Spatter cones, too, can be formed in cooling lava which still carries gas entrapped in it. When the gas finally escapes from the thickening molten rock, it pushes up some almost-hardened lava into small chimney-like cones that may be as high as twenty feet.

Imagine walking on such rough ground full of steep, jagged cliffs, ropy lava rock undermined by caves and tunnels, and almost-straight-walled spatter cones. You could easily think that you were walking on the surface of the moon. This was just what officials of the National Park Service imagined when they visited such an area near the town of Arco in Idaho. They set it up as a national monument, and called it Craters of the Moon National Monument. Here you can see, in a 75-square-mile area, some most unusual forms of cooled lava all bunched together.

Some basalt lava coming from a fissure flow can also harden into a strange form under certain conditions. As such a large lava surface

20

Ropy, or corded, lava in the Craters of the Moon National Monument.

Cooled lava often looks like sticky tar which was poured out of a barrel while still hot.

Craters of the Moon National Monument.

Devil's Post Pile, California.

Giant's Causeway, Ireland.

cools, it shrinks and cracks into six-sided blocks. Upon further cooling, the cracks extend deep down and a mass of six-sided columns of rock are left standing. You can see such *columnar jointing,* as it is called, in the Palisades of the Hudson River, along the Columbia River, and in the Devil's Post Pile in California. Across the Atlantic Ocean, in Europe, examples of columnar jointing are great tourist attractions. People travel many miles to see Fingal's Cave in Scotland, the Giant's Causeway in Ireland, and the columns of rock along the Rhine River in Germany.

A Glass Mountain, and Rock That Floats

IN THE northwestern part of Yellowstone National Park in Wyoming stands a mountain of black glass. It is made of a volcanic rock called *obsidian.*

Obsidian is made from granite-type lava that cooled very quickly — before its various minerals could separate out. While it is most always black, it can also be dark gray, red, or black streaked with red. American Indians prized such chips of rock from Yellowstone's Obsidian Cliff, for this material was the best to be had for arrowheads, spear points, knives, and scrapers. The Aztec Indians in Mexico, too, used obsidian found in their country. Although this glassy rock is found in other parts of the world, the greatest single chunk known is in our own Yellowstone National Park.

The same granite-type lava that makes obsidian sometimes makes a glassy rock so full of gas spaces that it is light enough to float. This spongy rock is called *pumice.* It looks like the frothy foam you see on the top of a pot of boiling soup or jam — indeed, it *is* frothy foam blown into the air from the top of boiling lava. As it was being ejected the lava foam cooled too quickly for the expanding gases entrapped in

Obsidian.

Pumice.

it to escape. They remained sealed in the rock in hundreds of tiny pockets, and they give the rock its porous, spongy appearance.

One story tells of a unique use to which pumice was once put because of its buoyancy. In 1883, the volcano on the island of Krakatoa erupted with a tremendous explosion. Almost two thirds of the entire island disappeared under the sea as a result of the blast. So much pumice was thrown into the ocean, that it covered the water around the island like a solid carpet. Sailors from a ship two miles offshore were able to walk the two miles, on a floating carpet of pumice, to what was left of the island.

Finely ground pumice makes a good gentle abrasive powder. It was used by dentists to clean teeth and by cabinetmakers to put a smooth finish on wood. Nowadays, although still called "pumice," a substitute is generally used for these purposes because the supply of natural pumice is running short.

Many forms of rocks and minerals result from volcanic eruptions — as we have just seen. Let us now turn to the forms of the volcanoes themselves.

The Shapes of Volcanic Cones

AT THE BEGINNING of this book, we said that a volcano is a mountain that "built itself." But we can also say that the shape of the mountain depends on what kind of material "built" it.

When an explosive eruption throws out mostly rocks, they soon pile up in a steep hill around the vent. Such a volcanic hill is called a *cinder cone*. Often lava flows later, cementing the loose rock into an almost perfect cone shape. This is just what happened when Paricutín was born. In fact, Paracutín is a perfect example of a cinder cone.

Active cinder cones have a short life — several weeks, months, or at most a few years. Because of this they rarely grow taller than 1,500 feet. Then, when they become inactive, rocks slide down into the crater and the vent becomes plugged. Except for its shape and its loose volcanic rock, you might never know such a mountain had ever been a volcano.

Quietly flowing lava builds up a mountain around the vent that hardly resembles a volcanic cone. With a flattened top and gently rounded sides, it looks like a great basin turned upside down. Such a volcano is called a *shield volcano*.

It takes many of these quiet lava flows, one on top of the other, to make a whole mountain. When you hear that the Hawaiian Islands are shield volcanoes — and that the base of Mauna Loa, the tallest mountain, is 16,000 feet under the ocean and almost 14,000 feet high — you can appreciate how many flows it must have taken to build such a volcanic cone.

The third and most usual kind of volcanic cone is the *composite* cone. As the name suggests, this type is made by alternate cinder-cone-producing eruptions and quiet lava flows. It is, therefore, made up of layers, or *strata,* of loose rock, now cemented, and hardened lava

Wenner-Gren Foundation

Cinder cones in Peru.

Mayon Volcano in the Philippines is a perfect composite cone.

Philippine Travel Information Office.

sheets. Because of this, such a volcano is often referred to as a *strato-volcano*.

Actually, the most beautiful volcanoes in the world are the composite or stratovolcanoes. Mt. Fujiyama in Japan, Mt. Rainier and Mt. Hood in the United States, are only some of these. Mayon, a 7,000-foot volcano in the Philippines, is considered the most perfect stratovolcano known.

Craters Vary, Too

REMEMBER that volcanoes have a crater at the top, connected by a vent to an underground reservoir of molten rock. It may seem strange, but the size of the crater has little to do with the height of its volcano. For example, one volcano in Hawaii is almost two miles high and its crater is twenty miles around the rim, or about seven miles in diameter. Yet another volcano, Mt. Orizaba in Mexico, is about three and a half miles high, with a crater less than a quarter of a mile across.

Perhaps the strangest kind of crater is a *caldera*. This type of crater is always very wide compared to its depth, like a shallow basin. Most geologists believe that a caldera is formed when the top of the volcano's cone collapses. In fact, you might call a caldera a "volcanic cave-in." This cave-in occurs when, shortly after an eruption, molten rock remaining in the vent sinks down, leaving a cavity under the cone. The top of the cone is often not strong enough to keep its shape without the lava to support it, and so collapses into the cavity underneath it. Volcanologists believe that most of the island of Krakatoa sank into such an undersea caldera when it all but disappeared in the 1883 eruption of its volcano.

Another well-known caldera is the bed of Crater Lake in Oregon, made after Mt. Mazama erupted thousands of years ago. The waters

Mt. Shishaldin in the Aleutian Islands has a very small crater.

How a caldera is formed. Left, side vents begin to drain off lava from central vent. Right, crater collapses as lava is withdrawn from central vent.

Crater Lake, a caldera, and Wizard Island, a cinder cone.

of this beautiful blue lake now cover the bottom of the caldera to a depth of 2,000 feet, and the remaining walls stand about 2,000 feet above the rim of the lake. In the middle of the lake lies Wizard Island, a younger cinder cone rising from the floor of the old crater. Thus visitors to Crater Lake National Park can see at first hand both a caldera and a cinder cone.

How Volcanologists Use Their Knowledge

PROBABLY the most important use that a volcanologist makes of his knowledge is predicting eruptions. By studying the kind of gas coming out of a crater while the volcano is not erupting actively, by measuring the temperature of the gas, and by observing the activity in the crater itself, scientists usually can warn the inhabitants of a volcanic area

29

when an eruption may be expected. Such predictions have saved many lives in Italy, Indonesia, Japan, and western Siberia. To help in research and to warn people of impending danger, volcanic observatories are maintained on Mt. Kilauea, on Mt. Vesuvius, and on many other active volcanoes. Sometimes volcanologists are able to save property as well as lives, as was done in Hawaii in 1935.

At this point, one thought may be puzzling you. If volcanoes are so dangerous, why do people live on their slopes, even when they can see steam escaping from the crater? There is a good reason for this: the soil made from volcanic rock is exceedingly fertile. Some of the finest vineyards in the world, for example, are located on the slopes of Mt. Vesuvius and Mt. Etna. Also, with proper advance warnings of eruptions, living in these areas has lost much of its terror.

People Make Use of Eruptions

ON THE ISLAND of Hawaii people rarely run away from eruptions of Mauna Loa and Kilauea. Instead, an eruption is a signal for everyone to come and see the spectacular sight. These two active volcanoes are considered so safe that their craters can easily be approached. Indeed, a whole tourist industry has arisen in and around the city of Hilo to accommodate those who wish to see the eruptions and to visit Hawaii National Park. Volcano House, the hotel within the park itself, is actually heated by steam piped to it from Kilauea.

Halfway around the world from Hawaii is Mt. Kituro in the Congo. The Africans living there take a most unusual advantage of the eruption of this volcano. When it is active, Mt. Kituro pours red-hot lava into nearby Lake Kivu, and after the eruption, the inhabitants of the villages along the shores of the lake sometimes go out in boats to collect half-boiled fish floating on the surface.

A very different advantage is taken of volcanic eruptions on the island of Stromboli in the Mediterranean Sea, near Sicily. The island rises sharply three thousand feet above the sea. It is the cone of a volcano which is continually erupting in small explosions, giving off showers of glowing rock. Since early days sailors have been using the light coming from its crater as a guide in navigation. Because of this, Stromboli has been called "the lighthouse of the Mediterranean."

One of the most interesting uses of volcanic material was first made in the province of Tuscany in central Italy. There hot steam rushes with great force from fumaroles and spouts high in the air. The people of the nearby town of Larderello pipe the steam into their homes for heat, as is done in Volcano House in Hawaii National Park. But far more important, steam from these "blowers," or *soffione*, is also used in connection with steam turbines and electric generators to generate electricity supplied to the cities of Leghorn and Florence, as well as to smaller towns nearby. In the past few years, New Zealand has begun to make use of fumaroles in the same way. Even more recently, in 1960, the fumaroles in Sonora County in northern California have been harnessed for power to generate electricity.

Hot Springs

ALTHOUGH hot springs are not really due to volcanic eruptions, we might consider them here, because they are so closely related to volcanoes. Hot springs are, in fact, water which becomes hot due to contact with magma. When these springs come to the surface of the earth, they often carry with them minerals which are considered by many people to make the water especially healthful for bathing. In addition, many doctors believe that the waters of such mineral hot springs help relieve arthritis and certain other diseases. The hot springs of Banff in

New Zealand National Publicity Studios

Natural steam is being piped to a generating station.

the Canadian Rockies, Hot Springs in Arkansas, and Baden-Baden in Germany are some of the most famous in the world.

Iceland has hundreds of hot springs. Most of the homes in the capital city of Reykjavik are supplied with hot running water and central heating by water piped to them from springs ten miles away. Hverdagerdi, thirty miles from Reykjavik, is known as the "hot spring town." In addition to its use in homes, this water is used to heat many greenhouses. In fact, the main industry in Hverdagerdi is the growing of flowers, vegetables, fruits, and even such tropical fruits as figs and bananas.

A Special Kind of Hot Spring

WHEN THE VENT through which a hot spring rises to the surface is crooked or partly blocked in some places, the spring behaves in a curious manner. Instead of flowing regularly and evenly, no water flows out at all for a time and then, suddenly, water gushes out into the air. It "plays" for a while like a fountain, then dies down again. Such a hot spring is called a *geyser*.

The irregular "plumbing system" of the geyser produces its action in this way: after a geyser has erupted the expelled water seeps down through cracks in the ground and back into the vent, or *feeding tube*. There the water remains for a while, and the lower part gets hotter and hotter from contact with hot rocks and magma. But since the feeding tube is partly blocked, the hot water at the bottom cannot circulate easily toward the top, as water does when a kettle of water is heated. In time, water at the bottom of the feeding tube reaches the temperature at which it would ordinarily boil. Yet it cannot do so, because of the pressure of all the water above it. For just as rock under pressure needs more than usual heat to melt, so water under pressure needs higher than normal heat to boil.

However, as contact with the hot rock continues, a little of the water finally reaches a high enough temperature to turn to steam. Now bubbles begin to rise and push the water column above, so that a little of the water near the mouth of the tube spills over. This makes the whole column of water lighter. With less pressure, more water turns to steam and more bubbles arise, pushing more water out of the tube. Again, the pressure becomes less, and still more steam is formed. This continues until the pressure at the bottom of the tube becomes low enough to allow this superheated water to turn to steam. Suddenly it does so, and explodes out of the tube, carrying with it all the water left above it.

How long a geyser "plays," how much water it expels, and how often it erupts depend on the depth, shape, and branches of its feeding tube. Some geysers rise only one or two inches, others hundreds of feet. There are some which erupt every few minutes, giving off a small

33

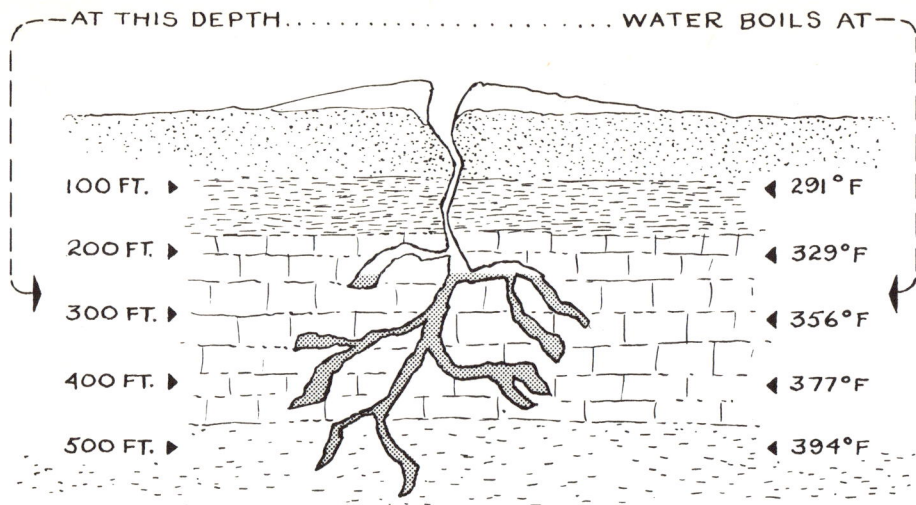

AT THIS DEPTH . . . . WATER BOILS AT

100 FT.	291° F
200 FT.	329° F
300 FT.	356° F
400 FT.	377° F
500 FT.	394° F

The "plumbing system" of a geyser.

stream of water; and some which erupt for hours, throwing out enough water to supply a town. While many geysers are unpredictable, others play so regularly that a schedule of their display times can be listed for visitors. The best-known of these is Old Faithful in Yellowstone National Park. It is so regular that an announcement is made over a loudspeaker a few minutes before it is due to play. Every 66 minutes it erupts, its water gradually rising about 150 feet into the air. Then it slowly subsides, and after a total of about four minutes, is quiet again, preparing for its next performance. No one who has seen the spectacle of Old Faithful in action can ever forget it.

Actually, there are many more geysers besides Old Faithful in Yellowstone National Park, since this region is the world's greatest geyser area. There are only two other countries where geysers are found in large numbers, New Zealand and Iceland.

Old Faithful geyser in eruption.

National Park Service Photo
Consulate General of Iceland

Piping natural hot water into Reykjavik, Iceland.

Witkind, U.S. Geological Survey
The Madison River Valley after the earthquake of August 17, 1959.

Earthquakes Can Change the Face of the Earth

THE Madison River flows out of Yellowstone National Park and into the state of Montana, where it later joins the Missouri River. Along its banks are a number of popular campgrounds used by people from all parts of the United States. But a visitor who had seen the Madison River or who had camped in Rock Creek Campground before August 17, 1959, would hardly recognize these places now. Rock Creek Campground is gone, buried under a landslide of rock which dammed the river and created a new lake.

A giant earthquake, occurring a little before midnight on that fateful August 17th, was what changed the face of the Madison River and its valley. "Earthquake Lake" has been added to the map behind where the campground once stood. Cliffs now rise where so recently the ground had been level, and a scar of bare rock marks the place where a 1,300-foot mountain face had broken off and crashed into the valley.

Elsewhere, too, earthquakes have changed the appearance of the land, although these changes are not often as spectacular as those in Montana. Along the coast near Japan, for example, earthquakes occurring over a period of two thousand years have raised the land only about forty-five feet. But near Yakatut Bay in Alaska, a series of earthquakes between September 3 and September 29, 1899 caused whole forests to be drowned beneath the ocean. Also, over a region including Missouri, Tennessee, and Arkansas, during the New Madrid earthquake of 1812, an area of 30,000 square miles sank as much as fifteen feet and Reelfoot Lake was formed. In addition, the ocean floor has had even more sudden changes than the land.

What causes an earthquake, and where are these tremblings of the earth likely to occur?

When the Solid Rock Shifts

IN TRYING to learn about the causes of earthquakes, geologists have experimented in their laboratories by placing rocks under various pressures. They have observed that under great pressure, the rocks gradually change their shapes. But, as the pressure builds up, the rocks cannot withstand the great strain upon them. They crack, or *fracture*, and shift their positions so as to relieve the strain.

This, geologists agree, is what happens in the underground rock to produce earthquakes, although they are not sure what causes these tremendous pressures. Seismologists — geologists who study earthquakes — know that most quakes occur in the crust, at depths ranging from five to twenty miles down. They know, too, that the shifting of the rock to adjust itself usually takes place along cracks, or *faults*, in

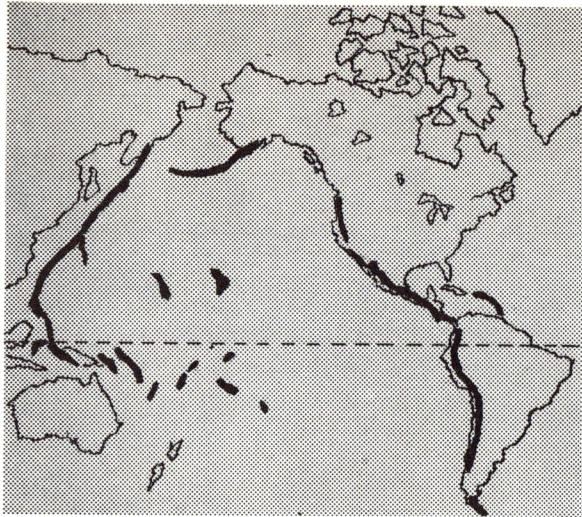

The earth's major earthquake zones.

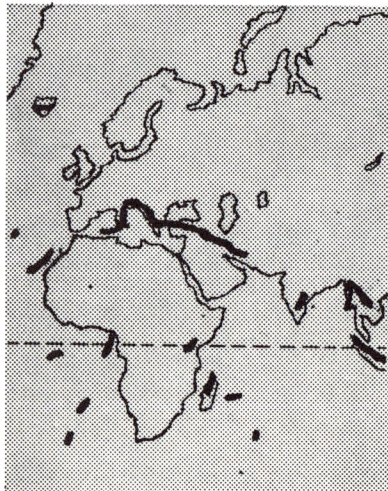

the earth's crust. These faults are likely to be found wherever there are very high mountains, especially if they are near deep seas.

Look at the accompanying map which shows the earth's two great earthquake zones. Do you notice that one of these is the same as the Pacific Belt of Fire? About four fifths of the earthquakes in the last twenty years have occurred in this Pacific Zone, both on land and on the ocean floor. Most of the others have taken place in an east-west zone that passes through Mexico, Central America, the Alps, the Mediterranean area, Greece, and the Caucasus Mountains in Europe. A large part of this zone is volcano area, too. In Asia, the same zone extends into Iran, the Himalayas, and Burma. There is also a small zone in the Atlantic Ocean, as the map shows; and again, volcanoes are found here. In fact, volcanoes and earthquakes are almost always found in the same region. Geologists think this is so because magma takes advantage of the weakness of the crust at these faults to break through to the surface.

There are altogether more than 600 earthquakes each year big enough for seismologists to take the trouble to locate, and thousands more so small that they can hardly be detected except by an instrument called a *seismograph* or *seismometer*. In order to understand how a seismometer works, we must first know something about earthquake shock waves and how they travel.

Shock Waves Set Off by Earthquakes

WHEN ROCK fractures or slips, three different types of waves are set up in the earth. Two of them are triggered at the same time — at the *focus*, or the point within the body of the earth where the break takes place. The third is started on the surface by the first two waves.

The two body waves that start at the focus travel through the earth

39

at different speeds. The faster one is called the *primary wave*, or *P wave*, because it arrives at the seismometer station first. It travels at the swift rate of five miles a second, pushing or compressing the rock in front of it. After it passes, the compressed material pulls back into place. This kind of wave is also called a *compression* wave, or a *push-pull* wave. A P wave can travel through any kind of material — solid, liquid, or gas.

The other body wave is called a *shear wave,* a *secondary wave*, or an S *wave,* and it is the second·one to arrive at the seismometer station. Instead of pushing rock ahead of it, an S wave shakes the rock at right angles to its path, as it travels along at three miles a second. An S wave can travel only through solid material. If it reaches a liquid, it becomes lost.

The third wave, the *long wave* or *L wave*, is a slower surface wave traveling at about 2½ miles a second. While it helps tell something about the violence of an earthquake and a number of other facts about it as well, it is of little importance in locating a quake. Seismologists use P and S waves to pinpoint a quake's *epicenter* — the place on the surface above its focus.

Now we are ready to learn how seismologists use these waves to study earthquakes with the help of a seismometer — or earthquake measurer.

The All-Important Seismometer

THE WORD *seismograph* comes from the words *seismos,* meaning "shake," and *graph,* meaning "write." It is, as you might therefore guess, an instrument that detects and makes a written record of the shaking of the earth. Nowadays it is more commonly called a seismometer.

The very first attempt to detect a distant earthquake was made about

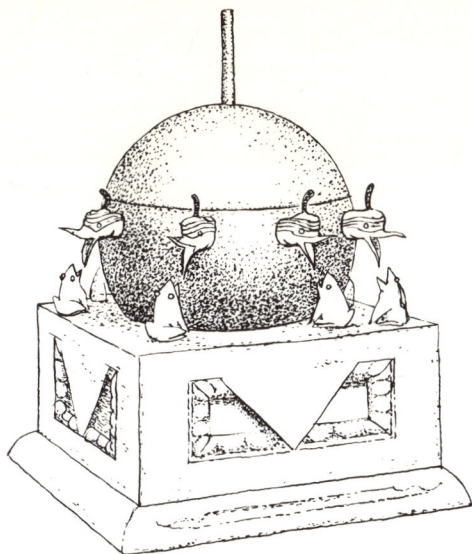

Choko's "seismometer"

136 A.D. in China by an inventor whose name was Choko. Choko's invention consisted of a large hollow ball standing on a base which was set on level ground. A heavy weight was suspended inside the shell. Around the large copper ball, at equal distances, were eight open-mouthed bronze dragon heads, and on the tongue of each was a small copper ball. A bronze open-mouthed toad stood beneath each dragon's head. The whole instrument was so arranged that, at the slightest jarring by an earthquake wave, the suspended weight would cause one of the balls to shoot from the tongue of a dragon into the mouth of the toad beneath it. Which little ball shot out depended upon which dragon head was nearest the path of the wave. True, Choko's device was not very accurate, but a crude record could still be kept of the occurrence and direction of a distant earthquake. A model of this first seismometer can be seen in the Earthquake Institute of the Imperial University of Tokyo.

41

Toward the end of the 19th century, the first true seismometer came into use. It had two parts. One was a heavy weight suspended by a wire spring from a frame firmly anchored to the bedrock. Attached to the weight was a fine-pointed pen. The other part of the seismometer was a revolving drum, also anchored to the ground. A sheet of ruled paper was fastened around the drum. The instrument was adjusted so that the pen on the weight just touched the paper on the revolving drum.

This was how the seismometer worked: as long as there was no earthquake, the pen left a fairly straight line on the revolving paper. But when the ground shook, the drum shook with it. The frame to which the weight was fastened shook, too, but the weight itself did not — for two reasons: first, the spring which supported it absorbed some of the "shake"; second, and more important, inertia kept it from moving. (If you know Sir Isaac Newton's law of inertia, you know that it takes a tremendous push to start a heavy object moving from a resting position.) The pen attached to the weight, then, did not move with the shaking earth, but the drum did. The mark made on the paper, therefore, was wavy and in step with the shaking of the drum. Here was a written record of an earthquake.

A modern seismometer is a little different, and more sensitive. Like the earlier seismometer, it too has a weight supported by springs from a frame set in a slab of concrete anchored to the bedrock. Again, when the bedrock shakes, so do the concrete and the frame, but the weight does not. Right under the weight are a pair of magnets firmly fastened to the frame, and of course moving with it. The weight itself carries a coil of wire whose ends are connected to a sensitive instrument called a *galvanometer*. This galvanometer, however, is different from the kind you may have seen, because it has a mirror instead of a pointer. A beam of light, as fine as a hair, constantly shines on its mirror.

The other part of the modern seismometer is the galvanometer and,

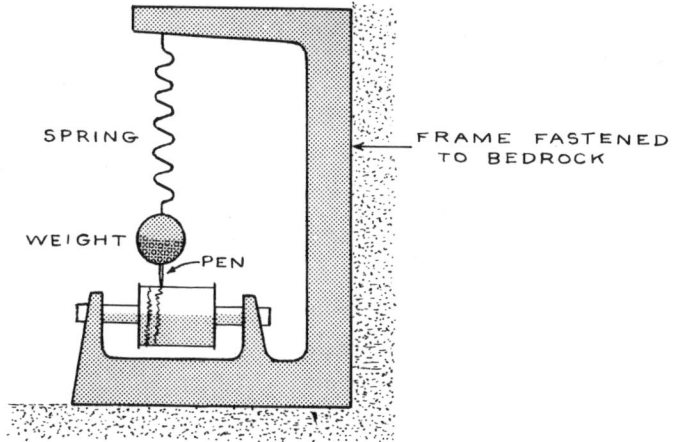

SPRING

FRAME FASTENED
TO BEDROCK

WEIGHT

PEN

Above, diagram of old-type seismometer. Below, diagram of modern seismometer.

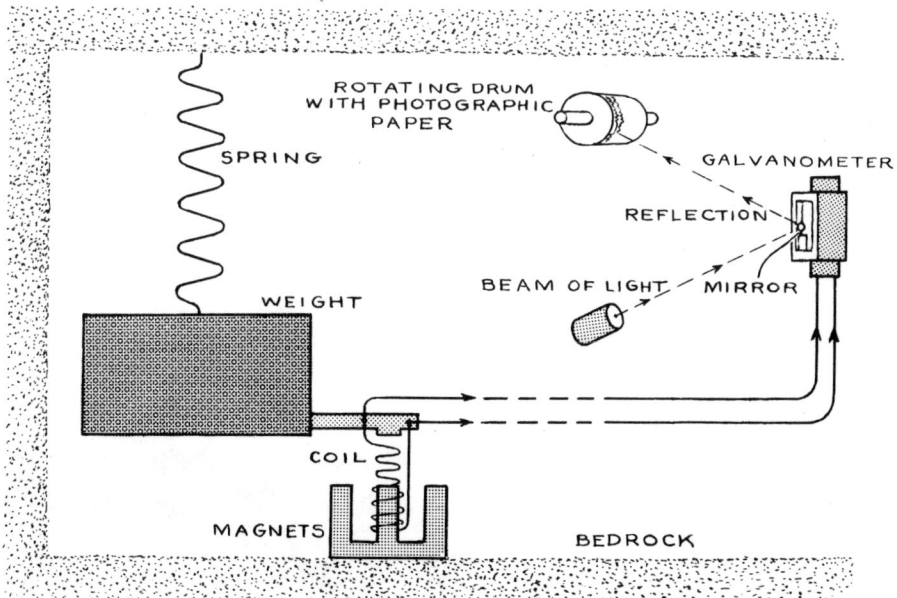

ROTATING DRUM
WITH PHOTOGRAPHIC
PAPER

GALVANOMETER

SPRING

REFLECTION

BEAM OF LIGHT

MIRROR

WEIGHT

COIL

MAGNETS

BEDROCK

at the proper distance from it, a rotating drum around which is wound a spool of light-sensitive paper. The galvanometer, the beam of light, and the drum with its paper must be in a dark room in which only a "safelight" may be used, but the weight and its frame may be in the light.

Whether there is a quake or not, the thin beam of light is reflected from the galvanometer mirror on to the photographic paper, leaving a line which appears when the paper is developed. As long as no quake takes place within the range of that particular seismometer, the line is fairly straight. But should a quake occur, a number of things happen almost at once: first, as the bedrock shakes, the frame and its magnets shake with it, but the weight and its coil are still. The magnets, moving near the coil of wire, generate a tiny electric current in the coil. This current is carried by the wires into the galvanometer.

Next, the galvanometer *amplifies* — makes larger — the tiny current so that it can move the mirror, just as it would move a pointer on an ordinary instrument. The light reflected from the moving mirror "jumps" with the mirror and leaves a jagged line on the photographic paper. If you have read the last few paragraphs carefully, you will see that the line left by the moving paper is in step with the vibrations of the bedrock. When the paper is developed, there is a record of the arrival of the P and S waves.

Seismometers are usually placed in a vault so that they can be easily anchored with concrete to the bedrock. Some of these instruments are so delicate that the crawling of a spider about the vault can show up on the seismometer record. Even the beating of surf against the shore of the continents causes a continuous tiny flicker of the light and leaves a mark on the paper.

Seismologists have made up a scale which they use to describe how violent an earthquake is. The records show that seismometers are dis-

Modern seismometer station.

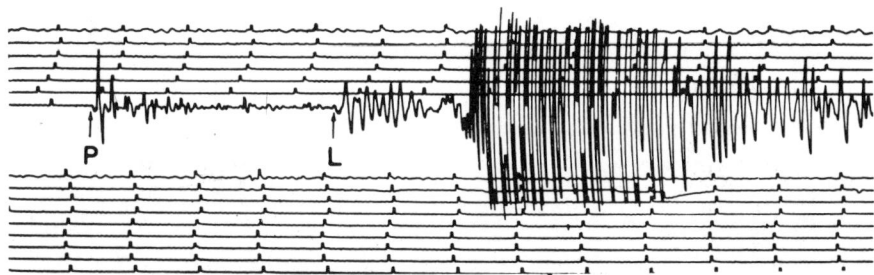

Hebgen Lake, Montana, earthquake, August 18, 1959. Recorded at Sitka, Alaska, approximately 1,325 miles distant.

Ocean bottom seismometer being readied for launching. Large sphere at right is marker buoy.

turbed about once every hour, but that large earthquakes occur every six or seven days. Since two thirds of them occur under the sea, and many of the others in uninhabited regions, a disturbance on a seismometer record is usually no cause for alarm.

Pinpointing an Earthquake

WHEN A seismologist wishes to locate the epicenter of an earthquake that has shown up on his seismometer, he cannot do this from the *seismogram*, or written record, alone. All the seismogram tells him are the times when the P and S waves reach his station, and how violent they are.

To locate a quake, the seismologist first finds the *difference* between the time of arrival of the P wave and that of the S wave. Let us suppose that an S wave reaches a station in New York on a certain date at 10:30 P.M., 4 minutes and 42 seconds after a P wave. The seismologist then refers to a table, which tells him that the epicenter is 2,000 miles away.

46

Although he has found its distance, he does not know its direction from his station.

Now he needs the cooperation of at least two other stations. Messages are sent, let us say, to a station in San Francisco and to another in Rio de Janeiro, asking for *their* distance from an earthquake that occurred on that date at eighteen seconds past 10:25 P.M., New York time. When the seismologist receives his answers, he learns that the epicenter was 3,800 miles from San Francisco and 3,500 miles from Rio de Janeiro. Using a radius representing 2,000 miles, he draws a circle around New York. Next, using the same scale, he draws a circle with a radius representing 3,800 miles around San Francisco, and a third one, representing 3,500 miles, around Rio de Janeiro. The three circles cross at a point near the Dominican Republic, as the accompanying drawing shows. And here is the epicenter of the earthquake.

Pinpointing the epicenter of an earthquake.

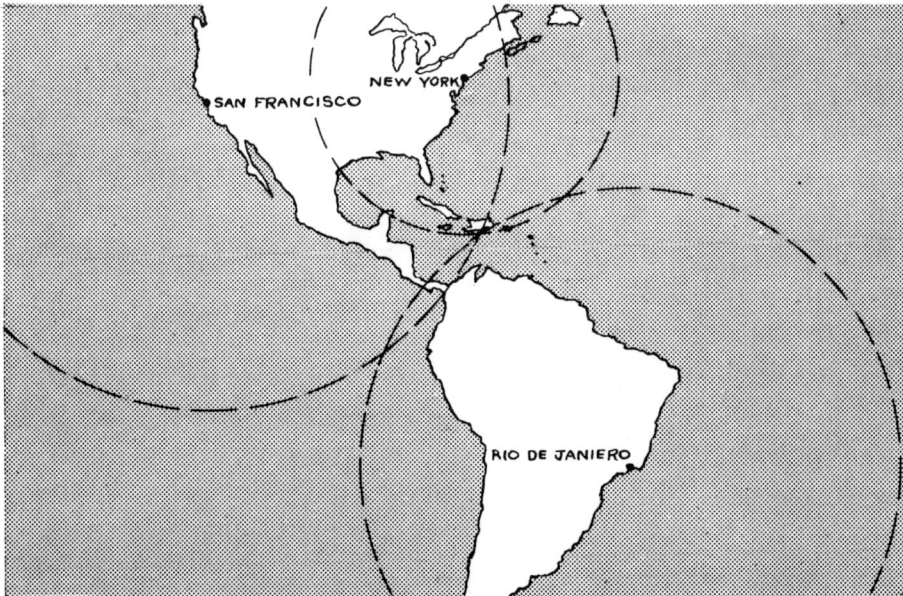

It is more usual nowadays for most seismometer stations to send their information regarding the distance of an earthquake to a central station. In the United States, these stations are maintained by the U. S. Coast and Geodetic Survey. There the circles are plotted and the location of an earthquake is found. This, as you can see, is a much more efficient way of pinpointing an earthquake.

Sometimes seismologists report an earthquake before news of it reaches the news wires. The majority of quakes, however, are never reported in the news at all, because they cause little or no damage to people and property.

The seismometer can locate earthquakes and tell us how severe they are, but even the most delicate instrument cannot *predict* one. In fact, no way has yet been found of telling beforehand that an earthquake is about to occur. Sometimes, a few minutes before a quake, a rumbling noise is heard, but there is never enough time to escape from the threatened area.

The only kind of warning that can be flashed from seismometer readings is the approach of a wall of water caused by an undersea quake. The name "tidal wave" that was once used for this kind of wave is not a good description of it, since it has nothing to do with tides. Now we use its Japanese name, *tsunami*. It is caused when the rock of the ocean floor breaks and a very long shallow wave of water is set up above the fault. As long as the wave remains far from land, it can do little damage because it is seldom more than a foot high. But a tsunami races along at 400 to 500 miles an hour, sometimes for thousands of miles, before it dies out. If it should reach a shore, the water may engulf it by piling up like a wall as high as a hundred feet. Fortunately, very few undersea quakes cause tsunami.

Until recently, the water along the shore gave the only warning that a tsunami was approaching. Just before the tsunami rushes in, the

48

water seems to be sucked away suddenly out toward the horizon. Now a distant seismometer station can send out a message of warning if necessary when a "seaquake" is detected. Seismologists are able to calculate how far and how fast a particular tsunami will travel, provided they know the strength of the quake and how deep the water is at its epicenter. They can then send a warning to a threatened shore, sometimes hours before the tsunami reaches it. While not much can be done to save property, such timely warnings have saved many lives.

A Seismometer Has Other Uses, Too

PREVIOUSLY in this book you read that by studying earthquake shock waves, scientists have been able to find out some things about the interior of the earth. Here is how they have done this:

Seismologists have figured out how deep down into the earth shock waves must go if they are to travel certain distances along the surface from the epicenter. They know, for example, that if the seismometer record farthest from the quake shows that an earthquake has occurred 1,500 miles away, the waves have penetrated 300 miles into the earth. If the epicenter is 7,000 miles away, the waves have penetrated 1,800 miles. But here is the important part. Beyond a depth of 1,800 miles, P waves slow down and change their direction, and S *waves disappear altogether*. At a depth of 3,160 miles, the P waves speed up again.

Remember, P waves travel through all kinds of material. However, they change their speed and their path when they go from one material to another. There must, therefore, be a different kind of material beginning at 1,800 miles below the surface. By their very disappearance, the S waves tell us that this material must be liquid — for S waves can travel only through solids. Careful study of the speed of P waves have shown, too, that the inner core of the earth, beginning at 3,160 miles

Burying a seismometer to help locate oil-bearing rock.

down, is solid, and denser than the crust and the mantle.

The seismometer is thus a very important tool for the geologist in studying the earth. But it also has other important uses in addition to helping us learn more about our planet. One of these is in prospecting for oil.

When a geologist suspects that an area has oil-bearing rock, he first has a number of holes about fifty feet deep drilled into the rock. Near-by are set special portable seismometers. Dynamite blasts are then set off in the holes, and the shock waves and their echoes created by the blasts are recorded by the seismometers. A geologist trained to interpret these seismograms can tell whether or not the rock is the kind that will be likely to bear oil.

Many scientists believe that another very important use of the seismometer is in detecting the underground testing of atomic weapons. They are almost sure they can now tell the difference on the seismogram between earthquake shock waves and those made by an underground nuclear blast. This, they claim, could possibly lead to an international agreement to stop all atomic testing.

50

When an Earthquake Strikes

IMAGINE the people in a city going about their everyday affairs, when suddenly the ground under their feet sways and shakes. They are hit by falling bricks and wooden beams as buildings topple over because these structures cannot withstand the strain of the shaking earth. Fires caused by overturned lamps remain unchecked, for panic has broken out in the city. Then, to complete the destruction, what is still left of the city is swamped by a great tsunami that rushes in from the sea.

All this was not imaginary to the people living in Lisbon, Portugal, on November 1, 1755. On that day, one of the greatest earthquakes in history occurred. Lisbon was at its epicenter, but more than a third of Europe felt the shock of this quake and of the "seaquake" that had caused the tsunami. Chandeliers began to swing in churches and houses a thousand miles away. The water of Loch Lomond in Scotland was agitated; in Amsterdam and Rotterdam, the water in the canals and rivers shook so that large ships snapped their cables. To add to the terror, November 1st is All Saints' Day, and superstitious people, not knowing the cause of earthquakes, thought the world was coming to an end.

Most people do not have such fears now. Some have even come to accept an earthquake as an ordinary occurrence, and hardly give it a second thought. This is true especially in the western part of the United States, along the San Andreas Rift. This rift is a valley half a mile to about a mile wide, starting just north of San Francisco and going for 600 miles in a southeasterly direction.

The San Andreas Rift is a fault in the earth's crust which has reached the surface. You would be correct in expecting many earthquakes along this weak spot. If you drive on a road along the rift, you can see where fences have been broken or twisted. You may be delayed, too,

51

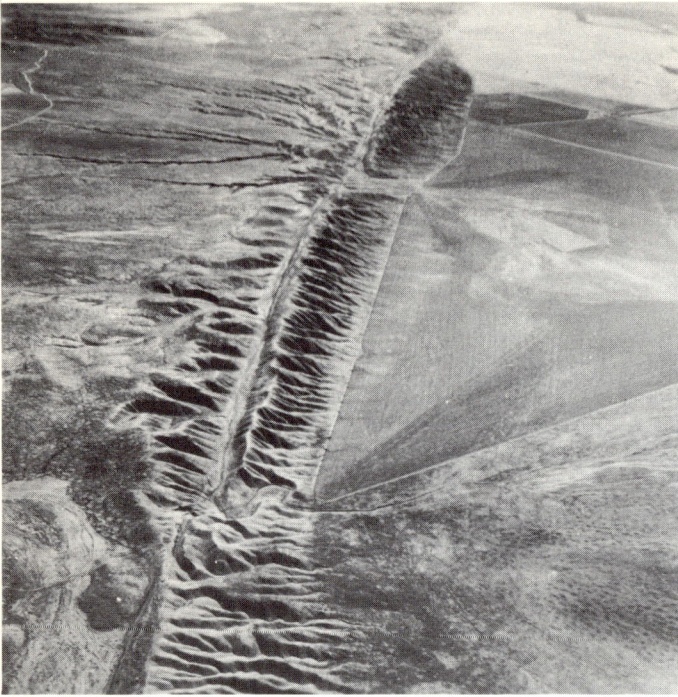

The San Andreas Rift as seen from the air.

Balsley, U.S. Geological Survey

Road shifted and broken by California earthquake in 1906.

Gilbert, U.S. Geological Survey

Cracks and fault made in the ground by the California earthquake of 1906.

Gilbert, U.S. Geological Survey

Stacy, U.S. Geological Survey

Twisted fence caused by 1959 earthquake in Montana.

by emergency road repairs made necessary when an earthquake caused a part of the road to drop suddenly.

Cracks have appeared in the ground and then closed up again, but in spite of some stories you may have heard, they have never "swallowed up" anyone. Neither has any other earthquake been known to open up cracks in the ground which "swallowed" people before they could scramble out. Yet, there is one true story of a cow that fell head-first into such a crack during an earthquake along the San Andreas Rift. Before the cow could get out, the crack closed up again, leaving nothing but the poor animal's tail sticking out of the ground.

The one really serious earthquake we know of in the San Andreas Rift occurred in San Francisco in 1906. Most of the damage to the city, however, was done not by the quake itself, but by fires started when gas lines broke throughout the city. Firemen were helpless in putting the fires out, because many water mains broke, and not enough pressure was left in those that remained to be of any use. When San Francisco was rebuilt, a system of valves was arranged to prevent water pressure from falling in parts of the city not affected by broken mains.

Architects learned some important lessons from the damage done by the San Francisco earthquake. One of these was put to use by the American architect Frank Lloyd Wright in an unusual way. This great designer of buildings was asked to draw up plans for a new hotel to be built in Tokyo. Wright submitted a design for a building with a steel frame that could sway with the bedrock if an earthquake should occur. He insisted that a large ornamental pool be built in front of the hotel, in spite of the owners' objections.

Shortly after this Imperial Hotel was finished in 1923, one of the severest earthquakes ever recorded rocked the city of Tokyo. Frank Lloyd Wright's building, like the very few others with steel frames, remained standing. Moreover, Wright proved how correct he was in

54

After the San Francisco earthquake of 1906.

insisting on the pool, for when a fire broke out in the hotel, there was plenty of water in the pool to put out the fire!

Wherever possible, today, buildings in an "earthquake zone" are designed to reduce earthquake damage. Top-heavy structures with thick stone or brick walls and heavy tiled roofs are avoided, because they collapse easily under the stress set up when the earth beneath them shakes. Instead, lighter-weight buildings are used, or tall steel-framed buildings are set deep in foundations in the bedrock or in concrete, as Frank Lloyd Wright did in Tokyo. Our American skyscrapers are good examples of earthquake-resistant buildings. We may not be able to avoid or control earthquakes, but we can prevent much of the damage they cause in our big cities.

Earthquakes and volcanoes are constantly at work. Together they have done much to shape the face of our earth. As far as we know, they will continue to change it as long as our earth exists.

Mt. Sakurajima, southern Kyushu, Japan, in eruption, 1946.

Glossary

BASALT — a dark, fine-grained heavy type of rock formed from cooled lava.

CALDERA — a large volcanic crater that is very wide compared to its depth; a volcanic "cave-in."

CINDER CONE — a volcanic hill made of loose rocks ejected from a volcanic vent, or from such rocks cemented together by lava flowed over them.

COLUMNAR JOINTING — roughly six-sided columns into which basalt lava sometimes cracks and hardens when it comes from a fissure flow.

COMPOSITE CONE — a volcano made of many alternate layers of cinders and hardened lava.

COMPRESSION WAVE — a "push-pull" wave, like a P earthquake wave, that first compresses the material in front of it and then allows the material to pull back.

CORDED LAVA — cooled lava rock hardened to look like thick cords or rope.

CORE OF THE EARTH — the 2,000 miles of the interior of the earth, closest to its center.

CRATER — the bowl-shaped depression, usually at the top of a volcano, which is connected by the vent to the underground magma.

CRUST — the solid first 20 or 30 miles of the earth.

EARTHQUAKE — the shaking of the crust of the earth due to the shifting of the rock to adjust to the strains on it.

EPICENTER — the place on the surface of the earth above the deeper focus of an earthquake. This is where the strongest effects of an earthquake are felt.

EXPLOSIVE ERUPTION — a violent eruption of a volcano.

FAULT — a break in the earth's crust, along which the rock has slipped, usually upward or downward.

FEEDING TUBE — the vent of a geyser.

FISSURE — a crack in the earth's rock, either on or below the surface.

FISSURE FLOW — a flow of lava, usually basalt, which comes from a fissure in the crust and spreads like a sheet over the land.

FOCUS — the point within the body of the earth where an earthquake starts.

FRACTURE — the breaking of the rock which makes up the earth.

FUMAROLE — a simple opening in the ground from which come gases and steam.

GALVANOMETER — an instrument used to measure electric current.

GEOLOGIST — a scientist who studies all about our earth.

GEYSER — a hot spring from which a column of very hot water is thrown at intervals into the air.

GRANITE — a light-colored, coarser-grained type of rock, not as heavy as basalt, formed from cooled lava.

LAVA — molten rock coming out of a volcano or fissure in the earth's crust.

LAVA CAVE — a cave made in slow-flowing lava when the crust hardened and the lava flowed out from underneath.

LAVA TUNNEL — an underground "tube" made in slow-flowing lava after the flow of lava stopped coming from the crater.

L WAVE — a long earthquake wave which travels along the surface of the earth; the slowest of the three kinds of earthquake waves.

MAGMA — molten rock, together with the gases it carries, while it is still underground.

MANTLE — the solid part of the earth just below the crust, which reaches to within 2,000 miles of the center of the earth.

MOLECULES — the smallest part into which a material can be broken down, and still keep the characteristics of that material.

OBSIDIAN — granite-type rock that cooled very quickly; volcanic glass.

PACIFIC BELT OF FIRE — the land bordering the Pacific Ocean, both east and west, where the world's greatest volcanic activity occurs.

PRIMARY WAVE — P wave, the faster compression wave caused by an earthquake.

PUMICE — glassy, granite-type rock, blown out during an explosive eruption; so frothy and full of gas spaces that it is light enough to float.

QUIET ERUPTION — a volcanic eruption during which lava flows gently out of the crater and down the sides of the volcano; a "Hawaiian type" eruption.

ROPY LAVA — another name for corded lava.

SECONDARY WAVE — S wave or shear wave, which starts together with the P wave at the focus of the earthquake. It travels slower than the P wave and is the second one to arrive at the seismometer station.

SEISMOGRAM — the written record made by a seismometer.

SEISMOGRAPH — another name for seismometer.

SEISMOLOGIST — a scientist who specializes in the study of earthquakes.

SEISMOMETER — an instrument used to detect an earthquake.

SHIELD VOLCANO — a broad, gently sloping volcanic cone made mostly of many layers of quiet basalt lava flows; Hawaiian type volcano.

SHOCK WAVES — waves set up in the earth's rocks by an earthquake.

SPATTER CONE — a small, chimney-like cone pushed up when gas escapes from thickening lava.

STRATOVOLCANO — another name for composite volcano.

THROAT — the upper part of the volcano's vent.

TSUNAMI — sometimes improperly called a "tidal wave"; a great wave of water, like a wall, caused by an undersea quake.

VENT — the opening, or "pipe," which leads from the crater of a volcano to the underground pool of magma.

VISCOUS — the condition of a liquid which has to do with its thickness. Viscosity is due to the tendency of a liquid's molecules to stick to each other. The more the molecules stick to each other, the less easily the liquid flows, and the more viscous the liquid is.

VOLCANIC ASH — solid pieces of volcanic material, up to one quarter of an inch in size.

VOLCANIC BLOCKS — large solid chunks of rock hurled from volcanoes during an eruption.

VOLCANIC CINDERS — sometimes used to mean ash and lapilli.

VOLCANIC DUST — fine powdery material ejected from a volcano.

VOLCANIC LAPILLI — little stones, larger than one-quarter inch in size, ejected from a volcano; usually about the size of a pea.

VOLCANO — a mountain which was built by rock material ejected from a vent leading to an underground reservoir of molten rock. When active, it expels hot rocks, lava, and gases.

VOLCANOLOGIST — a scientist who studies volcanoes.

VOLCANOLOGY — the science which deals with the study of volcanoes.

Index

Architecture and earthquakes, 54
Ash, 16
Atlantic Ocean, 10
Atomic weapons testing, 50

Basalt lava, 13, 20
Basalt magma, 12
Blocks, 16

Caldera (crater), 27
Caves, 20
Choko (chinese inventor), 41
Cinder cone, 25
Columnar jointing, 23
Composite cone, 25
Corded lava, 20
Core (earth layer), 4, 5, 6
Crater, 3
   types of, 27
Crater Lake, Oregon, 27
Crater Lake National Park, 29
Craters of the Moon National Monument,
   Idaho, 20
Crust (earth layer), 4, 7, 8

Diamonds, 16

Earth, 4, 49
Earthquake Institute, Imperial University
   of Tokyo, 41
Earthquake Lake, Montana, 36
Earthquake zones, 39
Earthquakes, 36-56
   and volcanoes, 39
   undersea, 48
Electric generators, 31
Epicenter, earthquake, 40
   locating, 47
Eruptions, geyser, 33

Eruptions, volcanic, 12
   prediction of, 29
Explosive eruption, 12

Faults, 37, 51
Fissure flows, 13, 20
Fissures, 13
Focus, earthquake, 39
Fumaroles, 14, 31

Galvanometer, 42, 43
Geology, 49, 50
Geyser, 33
Glossary, 57
Granite lava, 23
Granite magma, 12

Hawaii National Park, 20
Hawaiian Islands, 8, 18, 20, 25, 30
Hawaiian type of eruption, 13
Heat within the earth, 4
   its probable sources, 5
Hilo, Hawaii, 18, 30
Hot springs, 31
Hverdagerdi, Iceland, 32

Iceland, 13
   hot springs, 32
Imperial Hotel, Tokyo, 54
Indians, American, 23
Islands, volcanic, 8

Japan, 37

Kilauea, volcano, Hawaii, 30
Kimberly diamond mines, South Africa, 16
Kituro, Mount, Africa, 30
Kivu, Lake, Africa, 30
Krakatoa, 24, 27

Lapilli, 16
Lassen, Mount, California, 10
Lava, 2, 7, 12, 13
   flow, 17
   forms, 19-24
Lighthouse of the Mediterranean, 31
Lisbon, Portugal, 51
Long shock wave (L wave), 40

Madison River, 36
Magma, 7
   types of, 12
Mantle (earth layer), 4
Mauna Loa, volcano, Hawaii, 18, 20, 25,
   30
Mayon, volcano, Philippine Islands, 27
Mazama, Mount, Oregon, 27
Mediterranean Sea, 10
Melting, 5-7
Metallic deposits, 15
Mineral baths, 31
Molecules, 6
Mountains, 3

New Madrid earthquake, 37
New Zealand, 31

Obsidian, 23
Oil prospecting, 50
Old Faithful (geyser), 24
Orizaba, Mexico, 27

Pacific Belt of Fire, 10, 39
Pacific Ocean, 8, 10
Paricutín, Mexico, 1
Paricutín Volcano, Mexico, 1, 25
Pelée, Mount, Martinique, 10
Plateaus of lava, 13
Pompeii, 15
Pressure, 6, 7, 37
Primary shock wave (P wave), 40, 47, 49
Pulido, Dionisio, 1
Pumice, 23

Quiet eruption: *see* Hawaiian type eruption

Radioactivity, 5, 7
Reelfoot Lake, 37
Reykjavik, Iceland, 32
Rhyolite, 13
Rock, 37
Rock Creek Campground, Montana, 36
Roman mythology, 4
Ropy lava: *see* Corded lava

St. Pierre, Martinique, 10
San Andreas Rift, 51, 54
San Francisco earthquake, 54
Secondary shock wave (shear wave), 40,
   47, 49
Seismogram, 47
Seismograph: *see* Seismometer
Seismologists, *defined*, 37
Seismometer, 39, 40, 42, 47, 48, 49
   portable, 50
Shear wave: *see* Secondary shock wave
Shield volcano, 25
Shock waves, 39
   types of, 40
Sonora County, California, 31
Spatter cones, 20
Strato-volcano: *see* Composite cone
Stromboli, volcanic island, Mediterranean,
   31

Temperature of the earth, 4
Tidal wave: *see* Tsunami
Tokyo, Japan, 54
Tsunami, 48, 49, 51
Tunnel, 19
Tuscany, Italy, 31

United States Coast and Geodetic Survey,
   48

Valley of Ten Thousand Smokes, Alaska,
   14
Vent, 3, 12
Viscosity, 12
Volcanic belts, 8-10
Volcanic cones, 25
Volcanic dust, 16

62

Volcanic gases, 8, 12, 14, 29
Volcanic soil, 30
Volcanoes, 1-31, 39
Vulcan (Roman god), 4
Vulcano Is., Mediterranean, 4

Wizard Island, Oregon, 29
Wright, Frank Lloyd, 54

Yakatut Bay, Alaska, 37
Yellowstone National Park, 14, 23, 34